Democratic Rules of Order

Complete, easy-to-use
parliamentary guide for
governing meetings
of any size

Fred Francis
Peg Francis

Canadian Cataloguing in Publication Data

Democratic Rules of Order
Previous ed. has title:
Distinctly democratic rules of order
  Includes index.
  1. Meetings. 2. Parliamentary practice.
  Title: Distinctly democratic rules of order.
AS6D45   060.4'2   C98-901496-7
ISBN 0-9699260-4-9

First published in 1994
Seventh edition, fourth printing, June 2007
Printed on recycled paper

Published by Francis
Email: francis@democratic-rules.com
Website: www.democratic-rules.com

Distributed by
Gordon Soules Book Publishers Ltd.
1359 Ambleside Lane,
West Vancouver, BC, Canada V7T 2Y9
E-mail: books@gordonsoules.com
Web site: http://www.gordonsoules.com
(604) 922 6588 Fax: (604) 688 5442

Democratic Rules of Order

Contents

PART 1: The Rules

GOVERNING ELEMENTS

MEMBERS MAKING DECISIONS

KEEPING MEETINGS FLOWING

COMMITTEES AND SMALL MEETINGS

PART 2: Further Help

FREQUENTLY ASKED QUESTIONS

PART 1
The Rules

Introduction

Fairness and orderliness

These parliamentary rules of order help people to deliberate and consider ideas together, and then make decisions as wisely, fairly, and as easily as possible. Ideally, decisions are based on objective consideration of facts, unaffected by emotions, group pressures, or unnecessary protocols. The purpose of this book is to help your organization reach this ideal.

Democratic principles

This book is not an abriged version of other books. Its rules are determined by common practice and the natural laws of democracy, "rule by the ruled," as Webster's puts it. These self-evident principles, when applied to decision-making meetings, include

- **the right of each individual member** to participate equally and fully in orderly meetings that are free from intimidation, filibustering, and other disturbances and in which all members follow the same easily-understood rules, and the right to be equally and fully informed of all events, whether the member is present or not; and

- **the right of the majority of members** to make the decisions.

The seventh edition
The seventh edition, like each previous edition, has been revised to make the book clearer, more useful, and easier to work with. However, the rules of all editions are so similar that organizations can use earlier editions along with the latest edition without conflicts.

A democratic ideal
We should remember that we all belong to the same organization, with a common purpose. We can have widely differing views and still work together for a common good without dividing into opposing sides, each trying to get its own way. The best decisions are made when we listen thoughtfully to the information being presented and then make our own decisions privately.

Another democratic ideal
Must we accept a legal decision if it is a bad one? Yes and no. Yes, to practice democracy we must accept the decision and do what it requires us to do. No, we don't have to change our opinion. At some later date the opportunity may occur for a review of the decision, or we may even find that the decision was good after all!

Degrees of formality
In small or close-knit groups, decisions can often be made by consensus or general agreement, provided that the chair or secretary recording each decision is sure that most members agree (see pages 16 and 32).

Large groups, too, often make decisions informally. The mover's privilege (see page 19) allows co-operative members to work out decisions quickly and easily. A more formal amending process is automatically required if opinions are divided. The degree of formality is usually determined by custom, agreement, or a law as defined in the next paragraph.

Higher laws

Rules of order are automatically overruled when a law of the land, a constitution, a bylaw, or an existing standing rule applies. Throughout this book we refer to any of these as a law.

Rules of order apply to the conduct of meetings only. They do not interpret laws or make up for deficiencies in bylaws or standing rules.

For maximum efficiency

Sharing the decision-making process in meetings is like driving a car. There are rules to be learned and skills to be attained. Once this has been done, group decision-making is second nature, like driving. If each member reads this book thoughtfully at least once, and if the chair does the same at least twice, and if members agree to follow these rules, your meetings should move as easily as the car of an experienced driver who enjoys driving without wondering which pedal to press.

Electronic meetings

These rules can be used for telephone conference call meetings and for computer connected meetings in which discussions and voting are done electronically.

To adopt these rules of order

Add to the standing rules or bylaws a statement such as "This organization's meetings shall be governed by *Democratic Rules of Order*." You could also add "Members' general meetings shall be conducted by a formal chair, and the executive board's meetings shall be conducted by an informal chair" (see page 16).

An impersonal referee

These rules are complete. When adopted, they form the official rules of order for your organization's meetings. This book is your parliamentarian, or referee, when needed.

May this book help you and your organization to have productive and distinctly democratic meetings!

Fred and Peg Francis
Victoria, BC
Canada
March, 2000

Governing Elements
Good government has structure.

GOVERNMENT CONTROL
The governments of some jurisdictions require that the constitution and bylaws of incorporated societies be approved and that reports be submitted annually.

CONSTITUTION
A short document stating the name and purpose of the organization. To change the constitution may require advance notice, a large majority of votes (e.g., two-thirds or three-quarters), a secret ballot, and government approval. Indeed, some clauses may be unalterable, so the organization would have to be disbanded and reformed to change them. Many organizations today are formed without constitutions and place all governing rules in their bylaws.

BYLAWS
The governing rules of the organization, covering topics such as membership, officers, elections, duties, finances, meetings, quorum, discipline, amendments, and the seal. To change the bylaws may require advance notice, a large majority of votes (e.g., two-thirds or three-quarters), a secret ballot, and government approval.

STANDING RULES

Decisions that have been recorded in a list because they will be useful for future guidance. Standing rules can be changed by a majority of votes at any regular meeting, provided a quorum (see page 17) is present.

Unless all members are present and none object, changes to an existing standing rule governing the conduct of members' meetings apply only to future meetings. Some organizations require advance notice before a decision listed in the standing rules can be changed (see page 42, question 17).

RULES OF ORDER

A set of rules, established by the standing rules or bylaws, by which the members agree to govern their meetings. Rules of order are subject always to the laws of the land, the constitution, the bylaws and existing standing rules, any of which we call a law in this book.

EXECUTIVE BOARD

A group of members elected for a limited time to conduct the organization's business in accordance with the members' wishes. Their responsibilities and limitations are specified in the bylaws. Their authority lies only with the whole board, and no single member should assume any special authority or responsibility unless such powers have been delegated to that individual by the board. A title such as "Board of Directors," "Trustees," "Governors," or "Strata Council" does not reduce the need for their complete compliance with the will of the members.

OFFICERS
President, vice president, secretary, treasurer, etc., who have been elected by the members or appointed by the executive board for a limited time. Their responsibilities and limitations are specified in the bylaws. In some organizations, the officers form part or all of the executive board.

ELECTION PROCEDURES
Usually found in the bylaws and stating when elections are to be held, requirements for office, nominating and voting procedures, balloting, and number and appointment of vote counters.

Members Making Decisions

It is easier to make good decisions when everyone knows the rules.

FINAL AUTHORITY

Given a quorum, the will of the majority of members present and voting at any meeting held in accordance with the bylaws is the final authority and cannot be thwarted by any individual or by any previous decision, except where a law provides an exception.

EQUAL RIGHTS

Unless a law states differently, each member has one vote and an equal voice in all decisions.

THE CHAIR

The president or someone elected by the members or appointed by the executive board to conduct the members' meetings.

CHAIR'S AUTHORITY

The chair's duty is to preserve order and fairness in meetings by following the bylaws and rules of order. Members must abide by the rulings of the chair without debate except when a point of order (see page 29) is being used.

FORMAL CHAIR

In large meetings, the chair must be, and must be seen to be, absolutely impartial. The chair must refrain from expressing personal opinions in words or gestures and should not participate in discussion except to guide it in an orderly fashion. If, on rare occasions, the chair has relevant, brief information, the chair may depart from this rule, but the chair must always avoid showing any bias. The chair cannot make a motion.

If the chair needs to participate actively in a discussion, arrangements should be made for another member to fill this position until the motion has been voted on. A member may call the chair to a point of order for wrongful participation, and the chair should comply with good spirit.

INFORMAL CHAIR

In smaller or less formal meetings, members may have a bylaw, standing rule, or custom permitting the chair to participate in discussions with the same privileges as other members.

ADDRESSING THE CHAIR

Members must wait for permission (verbally or with a sign) from the chair before speaking. If several members stand at once, the chair selects one and notes who should be next. The others should sit until the speaker has finished, but in large assemblies the chair may require members wishing to speak to line up behind a microphone or put their names on a list and wait their turn.

QUORUM

The minimum number of members required by a law to be present before decisions can be made at meetings. The chair must find out if a quorum is present before the meeting begins and be kept informed of any drop in numbers that might cause the loss of a quorum. The chair should warn the members if this is likely to occur. If a quorum is not present the meeting may continue unofficially and should arrange, if possible, to get a quorum or to set the time of the next meeting.

AGENDA

The items of business and the order in which they are to be discussed at meetings, generally prepared by the secretary with executive board approval, or in smaller meetings by the chair. The agenda should be made known to members beforehand and can be changed by the members any time during the meeting except when a motion is on the floor. Agenda headings might include

- Opening of the meeting and approval of the agenda
- Minutes of the previous meeting
- Correspondence and reports
- Business arising from minutes, correspondence, and reports
- Motions to be presented and new business
- Announcements
- Adjournment and closing

MOTIONS AND DECISIONS

Sometimes decisions are made by consensus in which the Chair says "If there are no objections then [the decision is described]," but otherwise all decisions are made with motions or resolutions (see page 47, question 26) in which a member says "I move [that some action be taken]". Before any motion can be considered it must be seconded by another member; this prevents time being spent discussing an idea that has little chance of approval.

A new motion cannot be made until the motion on the floor has been withdrawn or voted on except for these motions, which directly affect the motion on the floor:

to amend (see page 20),
to postpone or refer (see page 21),
to change the voting procedure (see page 23),
to make a point of order (see page 29).

Unless a law specifically allows, a member must be present to make a motion, thus preserving the valuable mover's privilege. If the members have been notified already of a proposed motion, however, any member present can make the motion when it comes up on the agenda.

If the motion is clear, does not conflict with a law, and has been seconded, the chair or the secretary should read out the motion to make sure it is recorded correctly. Experienced movers sometimes have motions already written to give to the secretary. If possible, the motion should be word-ed affirmatively. It is customary to allow the mover to speak to the motion first and again at the end of the discussion.

A notice of motion to be presented at a future meeting can be made to members in writing or verbally during a meeting.

Special meeting: Unless a law states differently, a special meeting can make decisions only on topics stated in the notice calling that meeting.

A non-binding opinion poll (straw vote) can be held by the chair any time during the meeting if the members are willing. If a member objects, the chair should ask the members for a decision and conduct the opinion poll or not according to the members' vote (see page 47, question 27).

MOVER'S PRIVILEGE
During discussion, ideas for improving the motion may occur. Provided that not more than one member objects, the mover may reword or withdraw the motion any time before it has been voted on. A seconder for new wording or withdrawal is required. Rewording can be continued until the motion is as perfect as the mover, assisted by the meeting, can make it.

Once the mover has decided on new wording and it has been seconded, the chair or secretary should read out the reworded motion, which immediately becomes a new motion on the floor, replacing the

previous one. If two members object prior to this
reading out of the reworded motion, changes can
be made only with motions to amend.

AMENDMENTS

If the mover does not — or cannot, because of
objections — make a suggested change to the
motion, any member may move an amendment to
the original motion. An amendment may delete,
substitute, or add words that will modify the original motion but must not negate it or change the
topic.

The amendment, when accepted by the chair and
seconded, immediately becomes a new motion on
the floor, temporarily replacing the original
motion. It grants mover's privilege to the mover of
the amendment except that any rewording must be
acceptable to the chair as not changing the topic.
The details of the proposed amendment are discussed, not the original motion, and then the
amendment is voted on. An amendment cannot be
amended but can be defeated and replaced with
another amendment.

If the amendment passes, the secretary should
read the newly amended previous motion, which is
now a new motion on the floor to be discussed (if
desired) and voted on. It cannot be reworded or
withdrawn by the mover's privilege now, since it
has been partly established by the members, but
this new motion can be passed, defeated, or
amended again.

If the amendment fails, the previous motion again becomes the motion on the floor. If this previous motion was the original motion (having never been amended) then the original mover regains the mover's privilege. Further amendments are allowed, one at a time.

POSTPONE, REFER

A member may, any time before the motion has been voted on, move to **postpone** the motion on the floor (including any amendments passed) to an indefinite or a specific future occasion or to **refer** it to a standing or ad hoc committee for further study.

A member believing that consideration of a particular motion would be unwise could move "that we postpone the motion indefinitely." If the motion to **postpone indefinitely** is seconded and passed, then that particular motion cannot be discussed further at that meeting. It can be brought up at another meeting. A motion cannot be postponed permanently, because one meeting cannot bind a future meeting.

RESCIND

Unless a law makes an exception, and providing it would not create a breach of contract, a motion to rescind (repeal) a previous decision requires only a majority to pass and can be made at a time when the agenda allows (normally under new business or resulting from a point of order changing the agenda).

RECONSIDER

A motion to reconsider a previous decision can be made immediately after the decision has been made or at any meeting during new business or when it has been put on the agenda (perhaps by a point of order). It should be voted on immediately with little or no discussion. If the motion to reconsider is passed, then a member moves the previous motion or a replacement motion on the same topic and it is again discussed and voted on. The mover's privilege applies. The new decision replaces the previous one. A decision can be reconsidered as often as the members are willing (see page 60). Once the decision to reconsider has been made, no new business can be done until the reconsideration has been dealt with or the members have passed a motion to proceed with the agenda.

VOTING

When all members who wish to speak have done so, the chair should call for a vote. Unless a larger majority is required (see page 25), a decision is made (the motion is passed) when a quorum is present and more than half the votes are affirmative. Spoiled ballots and members not voting are not counted (see page 42, question 18).

Calling for a vote: Members who believe discussion is complete sometimes call out "question," or the chair might ask "Are you ready to vote?" The response is a guide for the chair only and does not force a vote. A member who believes that the chair is calling for the vote too early or is delaying too long can rise on a point of order (see page 29) and move that "we delay the vote for more discussion" or that "we vote now." Such a motion needs seconding and should be voted on with little or no discussion.

Member's right to speak: Every member has a right to speak once to a motion. The chair should not accept a motion to "vote now" if members who have not yet spoken are waiting to do so. In large meetings, however, if arguments on both sides of the question have been fairly presented and good order is being jeopardized by discussions becoming repetitive, the chair should accept such a motion.

After the members have decided to vote, either by general consensus or by passing a motion to vote, the chair or the secretary should read out the motion again, and the chair should make sure that all members understand it. Then the chair should call for the vote with "All in favor of the motion, please say 'yes' [or raise a hand]" (pause), "All opposed, say 'no' [or raise a hand]," or "Please mark your ballots now," etc. The chair must announce the result.

How votes are taken: Custom or a standing rule usually determines how votes are taken. Some groups vote by voice, which makes it more difficult to tell which way others are voting, and some by show of hands, voting cards, standing, secret ballot, or roll call (see page 46, question 25), which makes it easier to count the votes. If the chair, assisted by the secretary, is uncertain which way the vote went, the chair can ask for a show of hands. If it is still unclear, the chair can ask for a standing vote, saying "Those in favor, please stand" (pause), "Please be seated. Those opposed, please stand" (pause), "Please be seated."

A member who believes that there has been a **miscount** can ask—or, if necessary, move—"that we repeat the count with a standing [or ballot] vote." If this motion is seconded and passed, then the vote must be taken again. Motions can be made requiring that a vote be by ballot, that the counted ballots be destroyed, that the number of votes for and against be announced, or any other decisions the members wish to make.

Can a member vote without being present?
No, unless a law specifically allows proxy or absent voting.

Ethics: A member who would benefit personally from a decision may participate in the discussion but should voluntarily refrain from voting.

TIE VOTE
A tie vote means the motion has not passed. Members might wish to reconsider it immediately or at a future time. In some organizations, a law gives the chair an extra vote to break a tie.

LARGER MAJORITY VOTE

A mover who believes that the action being proposed needs strong support from many members may finish the motion with "and that this motion require a three-quarters [or some other ratio] affirmative vote to pass." Since a simple majority of members could easily remove this special ratio requirement with an amendment, this restriction, if not removed, has been accepted by the meeting and is now a requirement for the motion to pass. Sometimes a law will already exist requiring a larger majority vote in certain financial matters or bylaw changes, etc.

INFORMAL DISCUSSION

Occasionally there is merit in discussing an idea informally before a motion has been formulated. To allow for this a member may move "that we discuss [some topic] informally for a few minutes." This motion needs seconding and should be voted on almost immediately. After discussing the topic, if no motion is forthcoming, the meeting should proceed with the next item on the agenda.

MINUTES

Records of meetings kept by a secretary. They should include at least all major events and motions (see page 39, question 7). The secretary should maintain a filing system for minutes, reports, correspondence, etc.

After the minutes of the previous meeting have been circulated or read to all members, the chair should ask if there are any corrections. After any corrections have been made, the chair should ask "All in favor of adopting the minutes as circulated [or read, or corrected], please say 'yes' [or raise a hand]" (pause), "All opposed, please say 'no' [or raise a hand]" and then announce the decision. Once adopted, and signed by the chair and secretary, the minutes are an official record generally acceptable in a court of law.

REPORT

Executive boards, committees, and individuals often report to the members at meetings with information and/or recommendations.

After a report containing information has been read to the meeting, no motion is necessary. However, in some groups it is customary to finish with "I move that this report be **received** as read," which means that the members have heard and understood the report.

If the report contains a recommendation, the person presenting the report might move that "this report be **adopted** as read." This motion means that the members have agreed with and adopted the report and its recommendations. Of course, a member could propose an amendment changing "adopted" to "received" so that the members would not be bound by the report's recommendations. Treasurers' reports are usually received, rather than adopted, as the members are not in a position to guarantee the reports' accuracy.

ADJOURNMENT

If a bylaw or standing rule requires adjournment by a specified time, the chair should warn the members as it draws near, so that they can either finish quickly or extend the meeting with a motion, if it is allowed. If the meeting has not been extended, the chair should declare it adjourned at the specified time. Otherwise, the chair could say, "Since the business is finished, if there are no objections" (pause), "the meeting is adjourned." Or the chair could say, "Since the business is finished, let's adjourn; all in favor, please say 'yes' " (pause), "All opposed, please say 'no.' " If the motion passes, the chair then says "The meeting is adjourned."

Keeping Meetings Flowing

Good order in meetings is defined on this page.

STAYING ON THE SUBJECT

Members must discuss only one topic or motion at a time. If necessary, the chair should interrupt a speaker to insist that this rule be obeyed.

MORE THOUGHT, LESS TALK

A member must not take more than a fair share of floor time nor speak more than once on a motion until all others who wish to do so have had a turn. Exceptions may occur, however, with new information or a series of questions and answers involving useful facts. If necessary, members could pass a motion or have a standing rule limiting each speaker's time and appointing a timekeeper to enforce it.

MUTUAL RESPECT

Members must respect the rights of other members to their own quiet judgment on issues. Decisions should be based on consideration of the facts rather than on the skill of speakers or on an opinion of how others might vote. Members should speak to contribute light only, not heat!

Members must not use any form of personal criticism or ridicule to persuade a meeting. A member may criticize an idea but never a fellow member. A member must never interject or interfere with another member's right to an uninterrupted floor when speaking, except as allowed under a point of order. The chair should insist that this rule be followed.

POINT OF ORDER

A member who believes that a law or the meeting's good order is being breached may rise at any time and say, "Mister/Madam Chair, point of order." The chair should immediately acknowledge this member, who should then briefly explain why he or she believes a law or good order is being breached. The chair then rules on the point, either correcting the situation or explaining why it is in order.

If the chair declares that the situation is in order, the member may exercise **one last option** by rising and saying: "Mister/Madam Chair, I request a vote on this point of order." First the member and then the chair briefly explain their reasons. Then with little or no further discussion, the chair calls for a vote, saying "All who believe that [this action] conforms to our rules [or good order], please say 'yes' [or raise a hand]" (pause), "Those who disagree, please say 'no' [or raise a hand]." The chair and the member raising the point of order must abide by this vote.

DISTURBANCES

Filibustering or any other action that interferes with good order is not allowed. If a member is speaking too long, the chair should give a polite reminder. If the member continues, the chair can interrupt and request a decision from the meeting with "I request a decision from the meeting. All wishing this member to stop speaking now, please say 'yes' [or raise a hand]" (pause), "All opposed, please say 'no' [or raise a hand]." If the decision was for the member to stop speaking, the chair says, "Sir/Madam, the members wish you to stop speaking now. Please do so." Or if the decision was opposed, "Sir/Madam, the members are willing for you to continue. Please do so."

If a member or group of members does not stop speaking when asked by the chair or when a motion is passed by the members, then the chair can interrupt the speaker and ask for a motion requiring the speaker(s) to leave the meeting or, if necessary, for a motion to adjourn the meeting to reconvene at a later time. Only the members can make such a decision. Physical force should not be used against a member, although the speaker's microphone could be turned off on request of the chair (see page 36, question 2, and page 37, question 3).

DIFFERING OPINIONS

If there is a difference over the meaning of a bylaw or a procedure, etc., the chair may assist in solving the dispute. For example, the chair could pose a question designed to resolve the dispute and ask for a show of hands on it. The final decision rests with the members.

A NEW CHAIR

Serving as chair need not be a dreaded job, since these rules are straightforward and your fellow members can assist if needed. You can let it be known that you appreciate help. Ask members to call out if they can't hear you and to remind you if you forget something. Or you could suggest "If you see ways I can chair the meetings more efficiently, please ask the secretary to give me a copy of the rules of order in which you have highlighted the points I most need to review."

As well as studying the bylaws, standing rules, and rules of order beforehand, it is helpful to study the agenda and perhaps to write reminders and notes of things to say on it. By the way, starting meetings on time is a valuable habit.

Committees and Small Meetings

Meetings can be both informal and orderly.

COMMITTEES

Groups of one or more persons appointed by the executive board or the members to perform a continuing or short-term function. A **standing committee** is permanent until disbanded, although its membership may be changed periodically. An **ad hoc committee** is appointed to do a specific task and is temporary. The chair of a committee is appointed by the members, or the executive board, or elected from within the committee. Unless otherwise stated, the quorum of a committee or meeting is a majority of its members. Written guidelines are often used to provide order and continuity.

LESS FORMALITY

In committees and small meetings, the chair participates informally (see page 16) as a leader, subject always to the law and the will of the meeting, which in turn is responsible to the appointing body. Examples of degrees of formality include

(a) work parties making decisions by consensus led by the chair;

(b) small meetings making minor decisions by consensus that are announced by the chair and recorded in minutes;

(c) meetings of executive boards with an agenda and motions that are seconded, voted on, announced by the chair, and recorded in minutes by a secretary.

SPECIAL COMMITTEES

Most committees are democratic, but sometimes a non-democratic committee is formed in which one person has full responsibility, although others may help.

COMMITTEE MEETINGS

Ideally, a committee brings to bear upon a subject the combined experience and wisdom of several people. But sometimes well-meaning people talk too much or too forcefully, quite unaware of how much time this wastes and how unfair it is to the others. Meetings must be protected from such imbalance. The chair should not allow any member to be overly dominant.

The chair should assist members to stick to the business at hand. (Socializing can be done before or after the meeting.) Light good humor is great but should be brief. Replies to divergent opinions should be controlled and not allowed to degenerate into arguments. Let the facts speak for themselves. A little silence during a meeting with members pondering a situation could signify an effective group.

Most committees find that letters and creative concepts are better written and corrected by one or two people and then presented to the whole committee for final review.

In all meetings of any size, the ideal is members seeking the best answers together, not sides debating to have their own viewpoints adopted. (True for legislative assemblies too, if they only knew it!)

NON-DEMOCRATIC MEETINGS

Some meetings, such as a sales meeting in which a manager is instructing personnel, are not intended to be democratic – yet orderliness and respect for every individual, the basic principles of democratic rules, will improve the efficiency of any meeting. Including a little democratic decision-making, when possible, usually brightens a meeting and adds interest.

PART 2
Further Help

Frequently Asked Questions

INVOLVING THE CHAIR

Q1. What qualities does the chair most need?

A1. Self-control, good humor, and a thorough knowledge of the constitution, the bylaws, the standing rules, and the rules of order of the organization.

Q2. What can a chair do to ensure a fair and harmonious discussion of a contentious item?

A2. If necessary, the chair can remind members
- that the rules by which they have agreed to be governed allow them to discuss and make joint decisions in an orderly fashion, even when opinions are strongly divided;
- that a member's right to an uninterrupted floor includes freedom from any kind of audience response while that member is speaking;

- that a member who has spoken once may not reply to other speakers' statements, no matter how outrageous, until all others who wish to speak have done so;
- that a member must be acknowledged by the chair before speaking; and
- that we need not change our opinions, but we must accept the voting majority as the authorized decision-maker.

It may be helpful to have on hand copies of *Democratic Rules of Order* that members may borrow and return at the end of the meeting, so that appropriate sections can be referred to. If necessary, the chair should respectfully insist that these rules, especially those on pages 28 to 30, be followed.

Q3. **How should the chair deal with confrontational, angry members?**

A3. The most effective way is to not react even a little, to be calm, objective, proactive, and aware that remaining polite and dispassionate will help keep you in control. Compassion for people less able to control their emotions sometimes helps to keep you from dropping to the same level. It gets easier with experience.

Q4. Can the chair vote?

A4. Yes, unless a law states differently. However, a formal chair (see page 16) should do so as inconspicuously as possible to avoid showing bias.

Q5. If both the chair and the vice-chair are absent, what happens?

A5. Any member, perhaps the secretary, can call the meeting to order, call for nominations, and conduct an election of a temporary chair for that meeting.

Q6. Should the chair guide the discussion?

A6. An occasional verbal summary can be helpful but a formal chair (see page 16) must be careful to maintain impartiality. A chair who keeps the discussion on track, prevents overzealous members from dominating, helps members speak clearly one at a time, and keeps the meeting from dragging on with repetitions, is doing much to make the meeting worth while. Minor decisions can be made by consensus. For example, the chair might say, "Unless there is an objection, we will continue this meeting without the noisy microphone."

INVOLVING THE SECRETARY

Q7. How detailed should minutes be?

A7. As detailed as the secretary and/or the members wish. Minutes should contain all motions exactly as moved and a very brief description of all major actions. Minutes often look like expanded agendas. Minutes of formal meetings will generally be fuller than those of informal meetings. Minutes of informal meetings might be simply a dated list of events and decisions.

Q8. Must the minutes include the names of the mover and seconder?

A8. No, but in more formal meetings, the secretary may wish to include them, or the members could pass a motion requiring that this be done.

Q9. Must the minutes of the previous meeting be read at the beginning of the meeting?

A9. No. The members determine the agenda (see page 17). If the minutes have been circulated, the members may not wish to have them read aloud.

Q10. When minutes of the previous meeting have been corrected, must the secretary rewrite them?

A10. Normally corrections are made in the text or margin of the secretary's copy of the minutes and initialed by the chair and the secretary. However, if the secretary wishes, or if the members pass such a motion, then they should be rewritten or retyped and the new copy be signed by the chair and the secretary.

Q11. If the minutes of a previous meeting have been adopted and are later found to contain an error, what should be done?

A11. Since they have been adopted, that signed copy cannot be changed. The correction should be noted and approved by the members in the later meeting and included in its minutes. Then a note of the later correction should be made on or attached to the original minutes, dated, and signed by the chair and secretary.

Q12. Can a secretary make a motion?

A12. Any member except a formal chair (see page 16) can make a motion. However, in large meetings, it is usual for motions to be made from the floor.

ABOUT MOTIONS, ETC.

Q13. Can a motion be put on the agenda without naming a mover?

A13. Yes. When its turn comes on the agenda, any member can move it. If the motion is not moved, the meeting moves on to the next item on the agenda (see page 17).

Q14. What are the advantages of the mover's privilege (see page 19)?

A14. When members are co-operative, the mover's privilege enables them to improve a motion in an easy, natural way. Efficiency increases with experience. Since objection from any two members requires a more formal amending process, this privilege cannot be abused.

Q15. Can a member speak and vote against his or her own motion?

A15. Yes. The only restrictions on members' participation are those on pages 28 to 30. However, it may be wiser to modify the motion with the mover's privilege or an amendment (see pages 19 and 20).

Q16. Can a member who will be absent submit a written amendment to a motion that is on the agenda?

A16. No, unless a higher law (see page 10) states differently.

Q17. Can the members add or change a standing rule during the meeting to give the chair a tie-breaking vote?

A17. No, unless all members are present and none object. They can change the standing rule, but it will not take effect until the next meeting since the meeting is governed by the existing standing rules. This protects the right of members not present at a particular meeting from having a major rule changed during that meeting, when they are not there to participate in the decision (see standing rules, page 13, and tie vote, page 24).

Q18. Our quorum is forty. Forty members were present. On a vote there were eighteen affirmative votes, seventeen negative votes and one spoiled ballot that did not contain a "yes" or "no." Four members did not vote. Did the motion pass?

A18. Yes. Two conditions are necessary for a motion to pass:

    (1) the total number of members present must be at least a quorum; and

(2)   a majority of the votes cast must be affirmative.

In this case both conditions were met. A quorum of members was present. The spoiled ballot did not count. Eighteen votes was a majority of the thirty-five legitimate votes cast (see page 22).

Q19. What if a member feels an intermission would be helpful?

A19. The member can rise to a point of order and move that members take a break and reassemble at a stated time.

Q20. How could the agenda be changed during a meeting to have a particular topic considered earlier?

A20. At a convenient time, a member could rise on a point of order (assuming the proposed change will improve the good order of the meeting) and move the change in the agenda (see agenda, page 17).

Q21. When can a motion that has been postponed indefinitely be brought up again?

A21. In a future meeting at a time when the agenda allows (normally under new business or resulting from a point of order changing the agenda).

Q22. Our bylaws require a notice of motion
     in order to spend over $1,000 at any
     meeting. A notice of motion to install an
     electronic security system for $5,000 was
     properly sent to each member. During
     the meeting this motion was changed to
     purchasing better locks instead, for
     $4,000. Is this acceptable?

A22. Yes. The amount is within the financial
     limit established by the notice of motion,
     and the motion is on the same topic of
     security. If there were a difference of
     opinion on this, the chair could ask "If you
     agree with my decision to accept this
     motion as being in accord with the notice
     of motion, please raise your hand" (pause),
     "If opposed, please raise your hand," there-
     by emphasizing that the members are the
     final authority (see differing opinions,
     page 30).

     However, changing the motion, by means
     of the mover's privilege or an amendment,
     to purchasing a system for $5,200 would
     not be acceptable, as the amount is over
     the limit established by the notice of
     motion.

Q23. **How can we have a relaxed, interactive "think tank" session with maximum freedom to explore new, problem-solving ideas in an orderly way?**

A23. Use the informal discussion rule (see page 25) to free the meeting from formality. Then appoint the chair or a member to act as a neutral facilitator to be sure that every idea presented is received with complete absence of pre-judgment on its merit so that no one is reluctant to mention a "far-out" idea. You could also appoint the secretary or a member as a recorder to list the ideas on a board or chart so that none are lost.

Large meetings sometimes break into smaller groups, each with its own facilitator and recorder. When the session is finished, the groups come together and hear reports from the facilitators. Ideas from these sessions may lead to motions.

Q24. Can you give an example of an acceptable and an unacceptable amendment?

A24. Consider the motion "I move that we go to Sam's restaurant next time."

Amendment #1. "I move that we amend this motion by replacing the word 'Sam's' with 'The Golden Pagoda.' " This is acceptable, because it does not negate the motion or change the topic.

Amendment #2. "I move that we amend this motion by adding the word 'not' in front of the word 'go.' " This is not acceptable, because it negates the original motion (see page 20). The same result could be achieved more simply by defeating the original motion.

Q25. What is a vote by roll call?

A25. The secretary calls the name of each member, who then votes audibly. Each member's vote is recorded on a list.

Q26. What is a resolution?

A26. A resolution is a formal expression of the meeting's opinion on some topic, or a resolve to take some action worded in a special way. It usually consists of a preamble containing one or more premises followed by a conclusion. For example: "I move that we adopt the following resolution: WHEREAS [followed by one or more premises] THEREFORE BE IT RESOLVED THAT [followed by a resolve]." Of course, the members can change any part with the mover's privilege or amendments before voting on the whole motion.

Q27. What is an example of an opinion poll (straw vote)?

A27. While considering the purchase of a new computer, a member wanted to know how many members would make use of it and asked the chair to find out. The chair said "If there are no objections, we will have a show of hands on this question" (pause), "How many would use this computer if we buy it?" Then he announced the result. If a member had objected to this poll, the chair would have asked "All willing for this meeting to conduct this poll, please say 'yes' "(pause), "All opposed, please say 'no.' " The chair would then have conducted the poll or not as the meeting decided (see page 19).

Q28. **Can you give an example of how a higher law would modify a rule of order?**

A28. The rule on equal rights (see page 15) gives each member one vote. However, in some jurisdictions, laws governing meetings of condominium owners give each member one vote for each condominium unit owned by that member. A member owning five units in the condominium complex has five votes. Similarly in a corporation's shareholders' meeting, votes are usually proportional to the number of voting shares owned.

Another example would be the rule on a tie vote (see page 24). In some jurisdictions, laws governing meetings of condominium owners give the chair of the meeting a tie-breaking vote in addition to the chair's original vote.

Q29. **A motion was discussed, voted on, and passed by one vote. Immediately after, a member rose on a point of order and said that after reflection he wished to change his vote, which the chair accepted. This made a tie vote. When the vote was taken again, the chair, who had not previously voted, voted against the motion, thereby defeating it. Was this a correct, democratic decision?**

A29. Yes. It reflected the actual will of the
       majority of members (see final authority,
       page 15) and did not allow a procedure to
       thwart the members' true wishes. If
       objections are raised to a chair's decision, the
       members always have the last word, as they
       did in this case with their last vote.

**Q30. Will these rules work in conventions,
       conferences, and legislative assemblies?**

A30. Yes, they will work well in conjunction with
       the specific proceedures and rules dealing
       with agendas, delegates, speaking orders and
       limits, voting methods, and the many details
       necessary for the smooth operation of such
       events.

       It is easy to modify these rules of order with
       a standing rule or bylaw to make them
       conform to special needs.

Example of a Meeting Governed by These Rules

This script of an imaginary meeting contains examples of how the rules work in awkward situations. If you first read the rules and the questions and answers until you see that they are mostly common sense, this script will be more useful.

C: Chair

M: Members   Page reference

C: Welcome! Let's open our meeting. Are there any changes to the agenda? M1?

M1: I move that consideration of a fish pond be deleted from the agenda.

M2: I second the motion.   17

C: It has been moved and seconded that consideration of a fish pond be deleted from the agenda.
     [Discussion]

C: Are you ready to vote now?
      [Members call out "Question"]   22

C: Since we are ready to vote will the
secretary please read the motion.   23
      [Secretary reads the motion]

C: All in favor of deleting the fish pond
from the agenda, please raise a
hand…. All opposed, please raise a   24
hand…. Thank you. The vote is tied.
There are forty affirmative votes and
forty negative votes, so the motion did
not pass and the agenda remains
unchanged. The minutes of our last
meeting have been circulated. Are there
any changes or omissions? Yes, M3?

M3: *The meeting started at 7:30, not
8:00 p.m.*

C: Thank you M3. If there are no   18
objections (pause), will the secretary
please make that correction now. Are
there any further corrections?… All in
favor of adopting the minutes as
corrected, please raise a hand…. All
opposed, please raise a hand…. Thank
you. The minutes have been adopted as   25
corrected, and the secretary and I will
sign them now.

C:The next item on the agenda is a
      report from the executive board, to
      be read by M4.
        [M4 reads the report]

M4: *I move that this report be adopted*   26
    as read.

M5: *I second the motion.*

  C: It has been moved and seconded that
     the report be adopted as read. M6?

M6: *I don't think we should be bound by*
    this report's recommendation that we
    change our management company.
    I suggest that M4 replace the word
    "adopted" with the word "received."   19

  C: M4, are you willing to make that
     change?

M4: *No. I do not wish to make that*
    change.

  C: Yes, M6?

M6: *I move that we amend this motion by*
    replacing the word "adopted" with the
    word "received."   20

M7: *I second the motion.*

C: It has been moved and seconded that
   we amend this motion by replacing
   the word "adopted" with the word
   "received," to prevent the members
   from being bound by the report's
   recommendations.
      [Discussion]
      [Members call out "Question"]

C: If there are no objections, we will vote
   now. All in favor of the amendment
   changing the word "adopted" to the
   word "received," please raise a
   hand…. All opposed, please raise a
   hand…. Thank you. The amendment
   has been lost and now we must
   consider the original, unchanged,
   motion. Is there any further discussion?
   Since there is none, let's vote. All in
   favor of adopting the report as read,
   please raise a hand…. All opposed,
   please raise a hand…. Thank you. The
   motion to adopt has been passed.

M8: *Ms Chair. Point of order.*   29

  C: Yes, M8?

M8: *That vote was so close. I request we vote
    again by ballot.*

  C: I am satisfied the vote was correct.
     M8?

M8: *Well, I am not satisfied, and I move that we vote again by ballot!*   24

M9: *I second the motion.*

C: All in favor of voting again by ballot, please stand and remain standing until I say "thank you." Will the secretary please help me count?… Thank you. All opposed, please stand. Secretary, please help count again…. Thank you. The motion to vote again by ballot has been lost, thirty-seven affirmative and forty-three negative. So the original motion to adopt M4's report with its recommendations remains passed. The next item on the agenda is the fish pond. M10?

M10: *I move that we informally discuss the idea of a new fish pond for a few minutes now.*   25

M11: *I second the motion.*

C: All in favor of informally discussing the fish pond now please raise a hand…. All opposed please raise a hand…. Thank you. The motion has been passed, so we will now discuss this topic together informally.
[Informal discussion]

M12: *Since we are not ready to make a motion on this topic yet, I move that we continue with the agenda now.*

M13: *I second the motion.*

  C: All in favor of continuing with the
      agenda now, please raise a hand… All
      opposed, please raise a hand… Thank
      you. The motion has been passed. The
      next item arising from the minutes is
      the notice of motion made at our last   19
      meeting about painting our building.
      M14?

M14: *Because I believe this motion should*
      have strong support from a large
      majority of members, it contains a
      special condition. I move that we have
      all the exterior wood of our building
      painted at a cost not to exceed $5,000
      and that this motion require a 75
      percent affirmative vote to pass.   25

M15: *I second the motion.*

  C: Since members have been notified, this
      motion complies with our bylaws and is
      in order. Would the secretary please
      read it.
          [Secretary reads the motion]

  C: M14, do you wish to speak to your
      motion?
          [M14 speaks to the motion]
          [Discussion]

M14: *After hearing the discussion I wish to*
      reword my motion to read: that we have

*the exterior window frames of our
building painted at a cost not to exceed
$4,000, and that this motion require a
75 percent affirmative vote to pass.*

M16: *I second the motion.*

M17: *I object to this change in the motion.*

M18: *I also object to this change in the*   19
      motion.

C: Since there have been two objections,
    this motion cannot be changed with the
    mover's privilege, and the original
    motion is still the motion on the floor.
    M14?

M14: *I move that we amend the motion by
      replacing the words "all the wood on the
      exterior of our building" with "the
      exterior window frames" and the price
      of "$5,000" with "$4,000."*   20

M19: *I second the amendment.*

C: The amendment is in order. Would the
    secretary please read the amendment to
    be sure we have it written correctly?
        [Secretary reads the amendment]

C: The mover of the amendment may
    speak first.
        [Discussion]
        [Members call out "Question"]

C: Hearing no objection, let's vote now. Will the secretary please read the amendment?

   [Secretary reads the amendment]

C: All in favor of the amendment, please raise a hand…. All opposed, please raise a hand…. Thank you. A majority are in favor and the amendment has been passed. The newly amended motion is now the motion on the floor. Would the secretary please read this new motion?

   [Secretary reads the motion]
   [Discussion]

C: Is there any further discussion? Will the secretary please read the new motion again before we vote on it?

   [Secretary reads the motion]

C: Does everyone understand what we are voting on?… To make counting easy we will have a standing vote. All in favor of the motion, please stand…. All opposed, please stand…. Thank you. There were forty-eight affirmative votes and thirty-two negative votes, which means 60 percent are affirmative. The motion required 75 percent to pass. It has been lost. M20?   23

M20: *I move that we reconsider this motion.*   22

M21: *I second the motion.*

C: All in favor of reconsidering the motion, please raise a hand…. All opposed, please raise a hand…. A majority is in favor, and the motion to reconsider has been passed. M22?

M22: *With a slight modification, I think this idea might gain approval. I move that we have the exterior window frames and doors of the building painted at a cost not to exceed $4,500 and that this motion require a 75 percent affirmative vote to pass.*

M23: *I second the motion.*

C: Would the secretary please read the motion.
   [Secretary reads the motion]
   [Discussion]

C: M24?

M24: *Ms Chair, I move we vote now.*

M25: *I second the motion.*

C: As soon as M26, who was waiting to speak, has had his turn, I will accept your motion.

23

M26: *Thank you….*

C: It has been moved and seconded that we vote now.

M28: *Ms Chair, point of order. Several more of us would like to speak to this motion.*

C: Both sides of the question have been fairly presented during the past twenty minutes. Over eighty members are present. We will let the members decide. All in favor of voting now, please raise a hand.... All opposed, please raise a hand.... Thank you. The motion is carried and we will vote now. Secretary, please read the motion once again.

    [Secretary reads the motion]

23

C: Thank you. We will have a standing vote. All in favor, please stand.... Thank you. All opposed, please stand.... Thank you. There were sixty affirmative votes and twenty negative votes. The number of affirmative votes was 75 percent of the total votes and so the motion has been passed. The executive board can now have this work done. Next on our agenda is new business. M29?

M29: *I move that we reconsider this last motion.*

22

M30: *I second the motion.*

C: All in favor of reconsidering this last motion, please raise a hand…. All opposed, please raise a hand…. The motion to reconsider has been lost.

M30: *I move that we reconsider this last motion.*

M29: *I second the motion.*

C: This motion is out of order as we have already made a decision on it. M30?

M30: *Ms Chair. It is not out of order, as our rules of order state on page 22 that "A decision can be reconsidered as often as the members are willing."*

C: The members have just decided that they are not willing to reconsider this motion, and so we will now proceed with new business. M31?

M31: *My condominium is next to the games room, and players are frequently noisy. I move that this room be closed daily at 9:00 p.m.*

C: Is there a seconder for the motion? The motion fails for lack of a seconder. M32?

18

M32: *I move that we post a sign in the games room asking players to be quiet after 9:00 p.m.*

M33: I second the motion.

  C: It has been moved and seconded that we post a sign in the games room requesting players to be quiet after 9:00 p.m. Is there any discussion?

M34: *The motion should put a limit on the cost.*

  C: M32?

M32: *Good idea. I would like to change my motion to read that the maintenance committee be asked to spend up to $45 for a sign in the games room requesting players to be quiet after 9:00 p.m.*

M33: *I second the new motion.*

M35: *I object to this change in M30's original motion.*

  C: Since there is only one objection, this change is acceptable. Will the secretary please read the new motion.   19
        [Secretary reads the motion]

  C: M36?

M36: *Because there are other factors to be considered, I move that we refer this motion to the executive board for their consideration and ask them to report back to us at our next meeting.*   21

M37: I second the motion.
  [Discussion]

  C: Anyone else? It has been moved and seconded that we refer this motion to the executive board and ask them to report back to us at our next meeting. All in favor, please raise a hand.... All opposed, please raise a hand.... The motion is carried. Is there any further new business? M38?

M38: *Three meetings ago we decided to carpet the foyer. Nothing has been done. I move that we rescind the motion to carpet the foyer!*

M34: *I second the motion.*

M39: *Ms Chair. Point of order.*

  C: Go ahead, M39.

M39: *The contract has been given to a firm. By our rules of order we cannot rescind that motion.*

  C: I believe you are right, M39. We cannot rescind a motion if doing so would create a breach of contract. M38?

M38: *The color is wrong! The price is too high! We are not breaking a contract! It hasn't been signed yet! I insist that we—*

M39: *I agree with—*

21

C: Hold on a minute, M39! Please wait until you have been acknowledged before speaking.   16

M38: *Ms Chair. Point of order.*   29

C: Yes, M38.

M38: *I believe this motion is in order and request a vote on this point of order.*

C: Thank you, M38. Please explain your reasoning. Then I will explain my reasoning, and then we will vote.
     [M38 explains]
     [C responds]

C: Now the members will decide. All who believe that this motion to rescind is out of order, please raise a hand…. All opposed, please raise a hand…. Thank you. The motion has been carried. The motion to rescind has been considered out of order, and we will now proceed to the next item of business.
     [More business is discussed]

C: Our standing rules require us to adjourn by 10:00 p.m. We have only ten minutes left. M40?   27

M40: *I move that we change that standing rule to read: "that we adjourn at 10:00 p.m. or at a later time if the members attending so wish."*

M41: I second the motion.

C: This motion, if passed, will not affect tonight's closing time as we are governed by our existing standing rule. The motion before us is that we change our standing rule to read that "we adjourn at 10:00 p.m. or at a later time if the members attending so wish."

> [Short discussion]
> [Members call out "Question"]

C: Secretary, please read the motion.

> [Secretary reads the motion]

C: Hearing no objection, we will vote now. All in favor, please raise a hand.... All opposed, please raise a hand.... The motion has been carried and will allow members to extend the time of adjournment at future meetings. It is now 10:00 p.m. and I declare this meeting adjourned!

13

Calendars 1997 to 2099
to help plan events

To find which calendar to use for any date between 1997 and 2099, use the tables on the opposite page to find the appropriate calendar number. Then select it from the calendars below. Months with fewer than 31 days are April, June, September, and November, with 30 days, and February, with 28 days (29 in leap years).

CALENDAR C1

Mon	Tues	Wed	Thu	Fri	Sat	Sun
1	2	3	4	5	6	7
8	9	10	11	12	13	14
15	16	17	18	18	29	21
22	23	24	25	26	27	28
29	30	31				

CALENDAR C2

Mon	Tues	Wed	Thu	Fri	Sat	Sun
	1	2	3	4	5	6
7	8	9	10	11	12	13
14	15	16	17	18	19	20
21	22	23	24	25	26	27
28	29	30	31			

CALENDAR C3

Mon	Tues	Wed	Thu	Fri	Sat	Sun
		1	2	3	4	5
6	7	8	9	10	11	12
13	14	15	16	17	18	19
20	21	22	23	24	25	26
27	27	28	28	29	31	

CALENDAR C4

Mon	Tues	Wed	Thu	Fri	Sat	Sun
			1	2	3	4
5	6	7	8	9	10	11
12	13	14	15	16	17	18
19	20	21	22	23	24	25
26	27	28	29	30	31	

CALENDAR C5

Mon	Tues	Wed	Thu	Fri	Sat	Sun
				1	2	3
4	5	6	7	8	9	10
11	12	13	14	15	16	17
18	19	20	21	22	23	24
25	26	27	28	29	30	31

CALENDAR C6

Mon	Tues	Wed	Thu	Fri	Sat	Sun
					1	2
3	4	5	6	7	8	9
10	11	12	13	14	15	16
17	18	19	20	21	22	23
24	25	26	27	28	29	30
31						

CALENDAR C7

Mon	Tues	Wed	Thu	Fri	Sat	Sun
						1
2	3	4	5	6	7	8
9	10	11	12	13	14	15
16	17	18	19	20	21	22
23	24	25	26	27	28	29
30	31					

LEAP YEARS

YEARS	JAN	FEB	MAR	APR	MAY	JUN	JUL	AUG	SEP	OCT	NOV	DEC
2000, 2028, 2056, 2084	C6	C2	C3	C6	C1	C4	C6	C2	C5	C7	C3	C5
2004, 2032, 2060, 2088	C4	C7	C1	C4	C6	C2	C4	C7	C3	C5	C1	C3
2008, 2036, 2064, 2092	C2	C5	C6	C2	C4	C7	C2	C5	C1	C3	C6	C1
2012, 2040, 2068, 2096	C7	C3	C4	C7	C2	C5	C7	C3	C6	C1	C4	C6
2016, 2044, 2072	C5	C1	C2	C5	C7	C3	C5	C1	C4	C6	C2	C4
2020, 2048, 2076	C3	C6	C7	C3	C5	C1	C3	C6	C2	C4	C7	C2
2024, 2052, 2080	C1	C4	C5	C1	C3	C6	C1	C4	C7	C2	C5	C7

NON LEAP YEARS

YEARS	JAN	FEB	MAR	APR	MAY	JUN	JUL	AUG	SEP	OCT	NOV	DEC
1997, 2003, 2014, 2025, 2031, 2042, 2053, 2059, 2070, 2081, 2087, 2098	C3	C6	C6	C2	C4	C7	C2	C5	C1	C3	C6	C1
1998, 2009, 2015, 2026, 2037, 2043, 2054, 2065, 2071, 2082, 2093, 2099	C4	C7	C7	C3	C5	C1	C3	C6	C2	C4	C7	C2
1999, 2010, 2021, 2027, 2038, 2049, 2055, 2066, 2077, 2083, 2094	C5	C1	C1	C4	C6	C2	C4	C7	C3	C5	C1	C3
2001, 2007, 2018, 2029, 2035, 2046, 2057, 2063, 2074, 2085, 2091	C1	C4	C4	C7	C2	C5	C7	C3	C6	C1	C4	C6
2002, 2013, 2019, 2030, 2041, 2047, 2058, 2069, 2075, 2086, 2097	C2	C5	C5	C1	C3	C6	C1	C4	C7	C2	C5	C7
2005, 2011, 2022, 2033, 2039, 2050, 2061, 2067, 2078, 2089, 2095	C6	C2	C2	C5	C7	C3	C5	C1	C4	C6	C2	C4
2006, 2017, 2023, 2034, 2045, 2051, 2062, 2073, 2079, 2090	C7	C3	C3	C6	C1	C4	C6	C2	C5	C7	C3	C5

Summary of the Rules

Fairness (equal rights of members) and good order are the underlying principles (page 8).

The final authority is the majority of voting members, provided a quorum is present, subject always to any applicable higher law (a law of the land, a constitution, a bylaw, or an existing standing rule) (page 15).

In formal meetings, the chair guides impartially without taking part in discussion. In informal meetings, the chair participates as an equal member (page 16).

A motion should be worded affirmatively and must not conflict with any higher law. Each motion requires a seconder (page 18).

The mover's privilege allows the mover to reword or withdraw the motion provided there is a seconder and not more than one member objects (page 19).

Amendments can delete, substitute, or add words to a motion on the floor but must not negate it or change its topic. An amendment cannot be amended (page 20).

Postpone, refer: A motion can be postponed to an indefinite or a specific future occasion or referred to a committee for further study (page 21).

Rescind, reconsider: A previous decision can be rescinded or reconsidered by the members at any appropriate time (pages 21 and 22).

Voting: Common voting methods include voting by ballot, standing, show of hands, show of voting cards, and voice. For a motion to pass, a quorum must be present and more than half the votes cast must be affirmative (pages 22-24).

Informal discussion: A motion to informally discuss some topic, if passed, allows members to consider an idea without the formality of a motion (page 25).

Good order: Members should discuss only one motion at a time. A member must not take more than a fair share of floor time nor interrupt another member except as allowed with a point of order (pages 28-30).

Point of order: A member who believes that a law or the meeting's good order is being breached may rise immediately and say "point of order." The chair should allow the member to explain and, if necessary, should call for a vote for a decision (page 29).

Index

The Authors

Fred and Peg Francis have had decades of experience with meetings in school, college, business, church and community organizations as members and as officers. Peg taught in elementary schools and is an enthusiastic hobby painter. Fred taught mathematics in high schools and college and has designed several commercial products including clean-burning Seefire wood stoves, rodent-proof Speedibin composters, and children's Carpento building sets. He has degrees in political science and administration from the University of British Columbia. They live in Victoria, Canada, and have four wonderful children and six equally wonderful grandchildren.

This book has been a very satisfying project for Fred and Peg, who see the urgent need for more justice and stronger democracies in our world. For a democracy to work successfully the populace itself must understand and want to obey the democratic principles. Citizens need practice in making the individual rights of each member and the rights of the majority work together. People using this book are practicing and learning these laws, and helping the world at the grass-roots level.